BACH FOR THE YOUNG BASS PLAYER

Transcribed by
FREDERICK ZIMMERMANN

Piano parts by MIECZYSLAW KOLINSKI

ISBN 978-1-4234-0739-3

HAL•LEONARD® CORPORATION

7777 W. BLUEMOUND RD. P.O. BOX 13819 MILWAUKEE, WI 53213

Visit Hal Leonard Online at
www.halleonard.com

CONTENTS

BACH FOR THE YOUNG BASS PLAYER ⁸

Piano Parts by
Mieczyslaw Kolinski

Transcribed by
FREDERICK ZIMMERMANN

1. CHORALE

Dir, Jehovah, will ich singen
From the Notebook of
Anna Magdalena Bach

2. HYMN
Wie wohl ist mir
From the Notebook of
Anna Magdalena Bach

3. MUSETTE
From the Notebook of
Anna Magdalena Bach

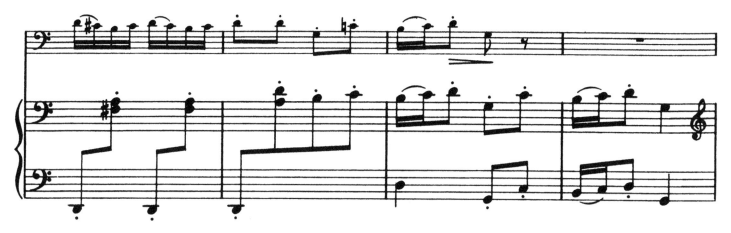

4. MINUET
From French Suite No. 2

5. POLONAISE

From the Notebook of
Anna Magdalena Bach

Allegro moderato

poco calando   a tempo

6. MINUET
From French Suite No. 4

Allegretto moderato

BACH
FOR THE
YOUNG
BASS PLAYER

Transcribed by

FREDERICK ZIMMERMANN

HAL•LEONARD®
CORPORATION

7777 W. BLUEMOUND RD. P.O. BOX 13819 MILWAUKEE, WI 53213

BACH FOR THE YOUNG BASS PLAYER

Piano Parts by
Mieczyslaw Kolinski

Transcribed by
FREDERICK ZIMMERMANN

1. CHORALE
Dir, Jehovah, will ich singen
From the Notebook of
Anna Magdalena Bach

Double Bass

2. HYMN
Wie wohl ist mir
From the Notebook of
Anna Magdalena Bach

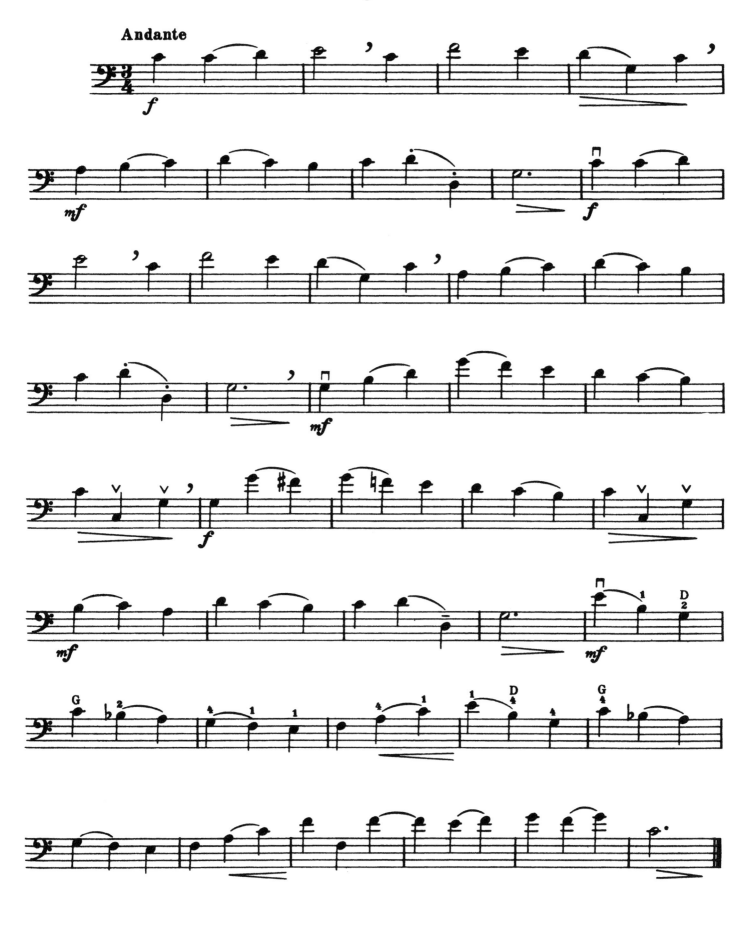

3. MUSETTE

From the Notebook of
Anna Magdalena Bach

4. MINUET
From French Suite No. 2

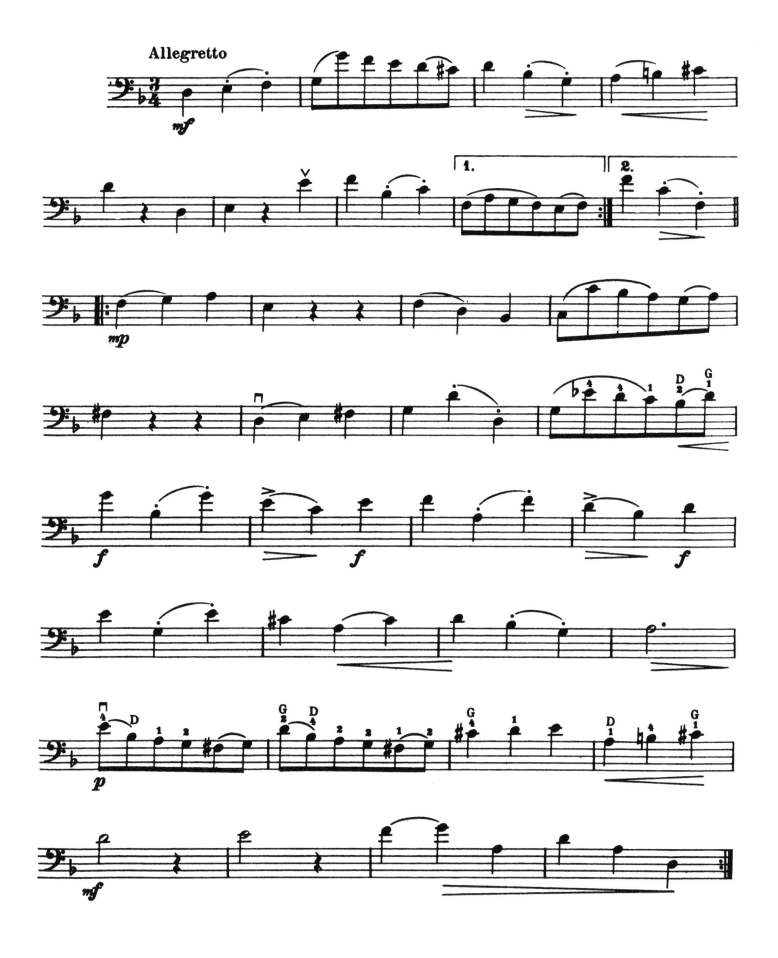

5. POLONAISE

From the Notebook of
Anna Magdalena Bach

6. MINUET
From French Suite No. 4

7. AIR
From French Suite No. 2

8. MINUET

9. MINUET

10. AIR

Warum betrübst du dich
From the Notebook of
Anna Magdalena Bach

11. SARABANDE
From French Suite No.4

12. PRELUDE
From Six Little Preludes

7. AIR
From French Suite No. 2

poco calando

a tempo

8. MINUET

Allegretto

9. MINUET

10. AIR

Warum betrübst du dich
From the Notebook of
Anna Magdalena Bach

11. SARABANDE
From French Suite No.4

12. PRELUDE
From Six Little Preludes